W9-ALM-026

The Western Wall

and Other Jewish Holy Places

Mandy Ross

Raintree

For information, address the publisher:
Raintree, 100 N. LaSalle, Suite 1200, Chicago, IL 60602

Design by Joanna Sapwell and StoryBooks
Printed and bound in China.

07 06 05 04 03
10 9 8 7 6 5 4 3 2 1

Library of Congress Cataloging-in-Publication Data

Ross, Mandy.
    The Western Wall / Mandy Ross.
      p. cm. -- (Holy places)
    Summary: An introduction to Judaism which focuses on some
significant and holy sites of the religion.
    Includes bibliographical references.
    ISBN 0-7398-6082-8 (HC), 1-4109-0055-X (Pbk.)
    1. Western Wall (Jerusalem)--Juvenile literature. 2. Temple of
Jerusalem (Jerusalem)--Juvenile literature. 3. Jerusalem in
Judaism--Juvenile literature.   [1. Western Wall (Jerusalem)
2. Judaism.]   I. Title. II. Series.
    DS109.32.W47R67 2003
    296.4'82--dc21

2002014390

Acknowledgments
The Publishers would like to thank the following for permission to reproduce photographs: AKG Photo pp. 6,
9; Associated Press p. 19; Christine Osborne Pictures pp. 20, 22; Circa Photo Library pp. 17, 21; Circa Photo
Library/Icorec p. 27; Corbis/Archivo Iconografico, S.A p. 11; E & E Picture Library p. 12; Getty Images p. 28;
Link Picture Library pp. 7, 10, 24; Photodisc p. 25; Popperfoto/Reuters p. 18; Powerstock Zefa p. 26; Robert
Harding Picture Library p. 8; Trip/A Tovy pp. 13, 14, 16; Trip/H Isachar pp. 15, 29; Trip/H Rogers p. 23;
Trip/R Seale p. 5.

Cover photograph reproduced with permission of Ords Eliason\Link.

Contents

Words printed in bold letters, **like this**, are explained in the Glossary on page 30.

What Is the Western Wall?

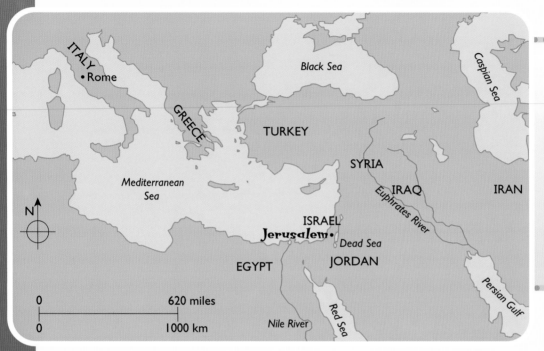

This map shows Israel and the countries of the Middle East.

The Western Wall is a holy place for Jews. It is in Jerusalem, a city in the modern-day country of Israel. Today, Jews from all over the world go to **pray** at the Western Wall. Many pray for peace, in a land that has seen many wars.

The Western Wall is all that is left of a great Jewish **Temple** in Jerusalem. The first Temple was built about 3,000 years ago by the Jewish king, Solomon. For over a thousand years, the Temple was the place where Jews went to **worship.** Twice, it was attacked and pulled down, but each time it was rebuilt. The Western Wall was one of the outer walls of the last Temple.

What is Judaism?

Judaism is the religion of the Jewish people. It is an ancient religion. Jewish people pray to one God, just as they did 4,000 years ago. They pray at the **synagogue** and read from their holy book, the **Hebrew Bible.** The **Torah scrolls** contain part of this Bible.

After it had been built for the third time, the Temple was finally destroyed in 70 **C.E.** by the Romans. It was never rebuilt so there is no Jewish Temple today.

Jerusalem is a **holy** city for three **religions:** Judaism, **Christianity,** and **Islam.** People from these religions have lived together peacefully there. But many wars have been fought over Jerusalem and there is still fighting in the city today.

The Western Wall formed part of the courtyard of the last Temple.

Why Is the Western Wall There?

Abraham was the first Jew. He lived over 4,000 years ago in the dry, desert land of the **Middle East.** At that time, the city of Jerusalem had not been built.

The **Hebrew Bible** tells how God called Abraham to a rocky mountain called Mount Moriah. There, God told Abraham to **sacrifice** his beloved son, Isaac. Abraham found it very difficult and thought it cruel, but because he loved and respected God, he wanted to obey. At the very last moment, God told Abraham to stop and to sacrifice a ram instead. Abraham had proved his love of God, and Isaac was safe.

This painting shows an angel stopping Abraham from sacrificing his son Isaac.

Desert mountains make up the land around Jerusalem.

The city of Jerusalem grew around Mount Moriah. Hundreds of years later, Solomon built his **Temple** on the spot where Jews believe God spoke to Abraham.

DID YOU KNOW?

The three religions of Judaism, **Christianity,** and **Islam** believe in one God. The story of Abraham is also told in the **Muslim** holy book, the Qur'an. In the Qur'an, Abraham is called Ibrahim. The Qur'an also says that God asked Ibrahim to sacrifice Isma'il, his other son, rather than Isaac.

Solomon's Temple

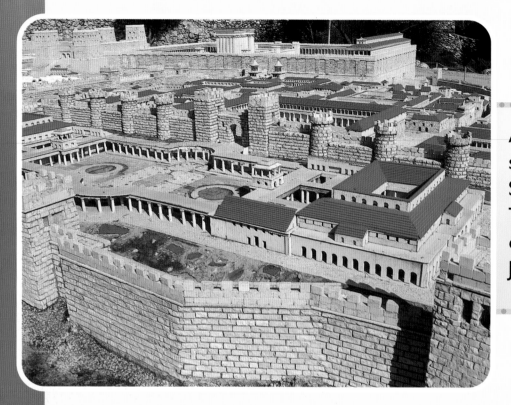

A model shows King Solomon's Temple in ancient Jerusalem.

In around 950 B.C.E., King Solomon built the first **Temple.** It was a huge and beautiful stone building, lined inside with fine wood. Every day early in the morning, priests led a procession to the Temple, to get ready for the morning **prayers.** The priests wore blue, purple, and scarlet robes. They were decorated with tiny golden bells and thread.

Inside the Temple was an ever-burning oil lamp called the Ner Tamid. It was a **symbol** of God's loving presence. In the most important part of the Temple stood the **Ark,** a special chest that held the Jews' **holy** books and writings.

The **Hebrew Bible** describes Solomon's Temple, how it was built, and what went on inside it. A Jewish **historian** named Josephus also wrote a description of the last Temple.

In 587 B.C.E., Solomon's Temple was destroyed by enemies of the Jewish people. Fifty years later, a new Temple was built, but it too would be destroyed.

The Western Wall was part of the outer wall of the third Temple. It formed a great courtyard where children went to school, and traders gathered to do business. This last Jewish Temple was finally destroyed in 70 C.E. by the Romans.

This Roman carving shows soldiers destroying the Jewish Temple and taking away the holy goods.

Jerusalem Through History

A medieval Christian mosaic shows the walled city of Jerusalem.

Jerusalem is important to **Christians, Muslims,** and Jews. Christians believe that Jesus Christ, their leader, died there on the cross and rose again from the dead to go to heaven.

For Muslims, too, Jerusalem is a holy place. Muslims believe that the **prophet** Muhammad (**pbuh**) traveled there. He made a miraculous journey from a place called Mecca. They believe that he was lifted up to heaven from Mount Moriah.

People of many different **religions** have lived in and around Jerusalem. Since the time of Abraham, Jewish people have always lived in the area. But most Jews were forced to leave from about 70 **C.E.** onward. Other people moved in and their families later became the **Palestinians.**

The "Wailing" Wall

Many Jews made a holy journey, or **pilgrimage,** to the Western Wall. They cried at the destruction of the Temple and **prayed** for a time when Jews could worship freely there, in a country of their own. That is why the Western Wall is sometimes called the "Wailing" Wall.

Over the centuries, Jerusalem has had rulers from different religions. The Romans ruled when the last Temple was destroyed in 70 C.E. In the 1100s and 1200s C.E., Christian **crusaders** fought to take control. Later, Muslim Turkish rulers called the Ottomans took over.

The Ottomans ruled for hundreds of years, until World War I (1914–1918). After that, Britain took charge of the area. Britain promised both the Jewish and Arab peoples their own countries in Jerusalem.

A painting from the 1300s shows Christian crusaders in Jerusalem.

What Happens at the Western Wall?

Every day, Jewish people go to the Western Wall to **pray.** There are separate areas for men and women to pray.

The Wall is busiest on Friday evenings and Saturdays. This time is called Shabbat, the Jewish Sabbath. Sabbath means "the day of rest and prayer." On Friday evenings, young Jewish people gather to pray and dance beside the Wall. This is a happy and festive time. Then, on Saturday mornings, Shabbat services are held there with singing, praying, and reading from the **Torah scrolls.**

People dance by the Western Wall on Shabbat.

Prayers on paper

If you look closely at the Wall, you will see slips of paper folded and tucked into the cracks between the huge stones. When they visit the Wall, many Jewish people write down prayers and wishes. They slip them into the Wall, in hopes that their prayers will reach God especially quickly from there.

On Mondays and Thursdays, **Bar Mitzvah** and **Bat Mitzvah** services are held at the Western Wall. When Jewish boys are 13 they can become Bar Mitzvah, and when girls are 12 or 13 they can become Bat Mitzvah. It means the boy or girl is starting to become an adult. This is a very special and exciting time for the whole family. A boy who became Bar Mitzvah at the Wall tells of his memories on page 16.

Prayers written on slips of paper are tucked between the stones.

Bar Mitzvah at the Wall

Shimon Lev, from Birmingham, England, held his **Bar Mitzvah** at the Western Wall. He talks about his memories.

My thirteenth birthday was during summer vacation, so we planned to go to Israel and hold my Bar Mitzvah service at the Western Wall. I was very excited. All my life, I had heard so much about Israel and Jerusalem! It was the first time I had ever been abroad, too.

I traveled to Israel by plane with my parents and my sister. Other relatives and friends from Britain joined us, as well as some cousins from Israel whom I had never met before.

A Bar Mitzvah service is held beside the Western Wall.

When we got to the Western Wall that morning, it was already very busy. Lots of other people were **praying** there.

My father led the service, and at last I was called to read from the **Torah scroll.** This was the moment I had imagined for so long. I read and sang in **Hebrew.** When I finished, everyone shook my hand and congratulated me.

After the service, I went right up to the Wall and slipped a note between the stones, with my own private prayers.

Afterwards, everyone came back to our hotel for a meal and celebrations. Every Bar Mitzvah day is special—but mine was extra-special because it was at the Wall!

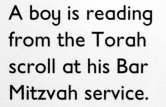

A boy is reading from the Torah scroll at his Bar Mitzvah service.

Other Events at the Western Wall

The Western Wall is the religious heart of Israel. Many special services and events are held there. People gather at the Wall for **prayers** and services to remember people who have died. In 1995, the Israeli Prime Minister, Yitzhak Rabin, was killed. Huge crowds gathered for a service at the Wall to honor his memory.

The Jewish calendar is based on the Moon instead of the Sun like the Western calendar. The months have different names. Tisha B'Av, the ninth day of the Jewish month of Av, is a sad day in the calendar. Jewish people remember how Solomon's **Temple** and the other Temples built in its place were destroyed.

These people are praying and studying at the Western Wall on Tisha B'Av.

Women of the Wall

Orthodox Jews are Jews who are very strict about keeping their religious traditions. Men and women must pray separately. In Orthodox Judaism, only men are allowed to hold and read the **Torah scroll.** A group called Women of the Wall wants women to have the same rights as men to pray at the Wall. They are asking for the right to hold and read from the Torah scrolls.

On Tisha B'Av Jews also remember other terrible events that happened to Jewish communities throughout history, including the **Holocaust.** There are special prayers at the Western Wall on Tisha B'Av. Some Jews fast to mark this sad day. This means they go without food or drink for a whole day and night.

Men and women pray together near the Western Wall.

Judaism Today

Jewish people believe in one God, just as they did in the time of Solomon's **Temple** 3,000 years ago. But since the Temple was destroyed, there have been many changes. Now, instead of a temple, Jewish people **pray** at a **synagogue.** Jewish leaders are called rabbis rather than priests.

Shabbat, the Jewish Sabbath, is a special day of rest. It lasts from sunset on Friday until sunset on Saturday. On Shabbat, many Jewish people go to the synagogue and spend time at home relaxing with their families. Many do not do any work during Shabbat. During synagogue services, the rabbi leads prayers and songs. There are readings in **Hebrew** from the **Torah scrolls.**

A rabbi is with the Torah scrolls in a synagogue.

Hebrew was the language that the first Jews spoke, long ago in the **Middle East.** Today, Jews everywhere still say prayers in Hebrew. Hebrew is written using different letters from English. It is written from right to left across a page, opposite to how English is written.

Jewish people celebrate their religion at home, too. On Friday nights, many families gather at home to light Shabbat candles and to share a meal together.

Judaism teaches people to lead a good life and to treat people fairly. Giving to charity and tikkun olam, which means "mending the world," are important beliefs.

People light special candles at home to welcome Shabbat.

What Is Inside a Synagogue?

Nowadays, **synagogues** are used instead of the **Temple.** Jewish people go to a synagogue to meet, **pray,** and learn. There are synagogues in most of the big cities around the world. Can you find out where your nearest synagogue is?

Most synagogues are built to face toward Jerusalem, where Solomon's Temple once stood. Synagogues contain things to help to remember the Temple. If you get the chance to visit a synagogue, look out for these things.

In the center of a synagogue is the Ark, where the **Torah scrolls** are kept.

Reading the Torah

The Torah scrolls are very important to Jewish people, who believe the scrolls should never be touched by human hands. Someone who is reading from the scrolls uses a special pointer shaped like a hand. This is called a Yad, and it keeps them from touching the scrolls.

In every synagogue, an ever-burning light called the Ner Tamid shines constantly like it did in the Temple. The Ner Tamid is kept lit to remind people that God is always there.

The Torah scrolls are kept in the **Ark,** a special cupboard or chest. This is a reminder of the Ark in the Temple. The scrolls themselves are draped in decorated robes, with tinkling silver bells on the top. These help people to remember the robes worn by the priests in the times of the Temple.

The Ark keeps the Torah scrolls safe.

23

Festivals at the Temple

Many Jewish festivals celebrated today remind the Jews of the **Temple** in ancient times.

Hanukkah, the festival of lights, comes in November or December. At Hanukkah, Jews remember how enemy soldiers were sent by King Antiochus of Syria to capture the Temple in the 100s B.C.E. The soldiers made the Temple **unholy** by putting up statues of the Greek god Zeus.

A small band of Jewish fighters defeated the large enemy army. They won back the Temple. They threw out the statues of Zeus and made the Temple holy again. But they could only find one small flask of oil to burn in the everlasting lamp.

People light candles at Hanukkah.

Pilgrimage to the Temple

In ancient times, Jews made a holy journey or **pilgrimage** to the Temple three times a year: at **Passover** in the spring, **Shavuot** in the early summer, and Sukkot, the harvest festival in the autumn.

For each of these festivals, hundreds of thousands of pilgrims traveled great distances to the Temple, bringing gifts with them. Huge crowds gathered to join in the **prayers** and celebrations. These festivals are still celebrated today.

A painting shows pilgrims visiting the Western Wall a long time ago.

Jews believe that God sent a **miracle** to keep the everlasting lamp lit for eight days, until fresh supplies of oil could be found.

Today at Hanukkah, Jewish people light candles every night for eight days to remember the miracle.

Jewish Festivals Today

Rosh Hashanah is the Jewish New Year. It falls in September or October. At Rosh Hashanah, there are **prayers** in the **synagogue.** The rabbi blows the shofar, a ram's horn, to welcome in the New Year. At Rosh Hashanah, Jews eat apples dipped in honey as they pray for a sweet New Year.

Yom Kippur means "Day of Atonement." It comes ten days after Rosh Hashanah. For a whole night and day, Jewish people go without food and drink. They pray and ask God's forgiveness for all bad things they have done during the year.

This rabbi is blowing a shofar at the Western Wall.

You can see the flat, square matzah bread on the table at a Passover meal.

Passover is a celebration of the Jews' escape from slavery in Egypt in ancient times. Today, families gather together at a Passover meal to retell the story.

The Jews fled so quickly from their homes, they did not have time to bake their bread properly. Instead, they ate very thin, flat bread baked in the hot sun as they traveled. This bread is called matzah. Jews eat matzah and other special foods to help them remember the story of Passover.

DID YOU KNOW?

At Easter, **Christians** remember how Jesus went to his Passover meal, the Last Supper, before he died the next day. That is why Passover and Easter are close together in the spring. At Easter, Christians remember how Jesus died on the cross, and how he rose from the dead.

Other Important Jewish Places

Masada is a mountain in the desert, a few hours' drive south of Jerusalem. It is about 1,300 feet (400 meters) high, with steep cliffs on all sides. It is a place that is hard to attack. The Romans had a camp at Masada, but in 66 C.E. Jewish fighters managed to capture it. They were fighting against the harsh rule of the Romans.

After the **Temple** was destroyed in 70 C.E., many Jews fled to Masada for safety. About a thousand Jewish people made their home there on top of the mountain.

This picture looks down on the ruins of Masada.

A memorial at Yad Vashem remembers Jews who were killed in the Holocaust.

The Romans started to build a huge ramp up one of the mountain sides. The ramp took two years to build. They then dragged their weapons up the ramp to fight the Jews.

At last, the Romans reached the top of the mountain. Rather than be killed or become slaves, all the Jews decided to kill themselves. In all, 960 men, women, and children died. Jewish people visit Masada today to remember the people who died there for their beliefs.

Yad Vashem

Yad Vashem is a museum and a memorial in Israel. It remembers the 6 million Jewish people who were killed by Adolf Hitler and his followers during the **Holocaust**. It also remembers people of other religions who helped Jews to survive during this terrible time. Yad Vashem is a painful place to visit, but it is important not to forget those who died.

Glossary

Ark special cupboard or chest for keeping holy books and scrolls in the Temple and in synagogues

Bar Mitzvah/Bat Mitzvah Hebrew for "Son of the Commandment"/ "Daughter of the Commandment." Becoming Bar or Bat Mitzvah means you are starting to be a Jewish grown-up.

B.C.E. stands for "Before the Common Era." People can use this rather than the Christian B.C., which counts up to the birth of Jesus. The year numbers are not changed.

C.E. stands for the "Common Era" instead of the Christian A.D. The year numbers are not changed.

Christian someone who follows the religion of Christianity, based on the teachings of Jesus

crusaders Christians from Europe who wanted to bring Jerusalem under Christian rule

Hebrew language that the first Jews spoke. Jews all around the world say prayers in Hebrew.

Hebrew Bible Jewish holy book.

historian someone who studies the past

Holocaust the murder of Jews by Adolf Hitler and his followers during the Second World War (1939 to 1945)

holy (unholy) to do with God. (Unholy means not to do with God.)

Islam religion followed by Muslims

Middle East   lands southeast of the Mediterranean Sea, including Israel, Egypt, Saudi Arabia, Iran, and Iraq

miracle   something that God made happen

Muslim   someone who follows the religion of Islam. Muslims pray to one God, whom they call Allah.

Orthodox   Orthodox Jews keep their traditions strictly without changing them

Palestinians   people who are not Jewish and have been living in Israel for 2,000 years

Passover   Jewish festival remembering how God helped the Jews to escape from slavery

pbuh   letters stand for "peace be upon him." It is always written after Mohammad's name.

pilgrimage   journey made for religious reasons

pray/prayer   to think about or talk to God. A prayer is the words you think or say when you pray.

prophet   someone who tells people what God wants

religions   belief in God or gods

sacred   another word for holy

sacrifice   to give up something to God

Shavuot   Jewish festival remembering how God gave the Torah to the prophet Moses

symbol   sign, or something that stands for something else

synagogue   where Jewish people go to meet, pray, and learn

temple   place of worship

Torah scrolls   long rolls of parchment with the words of the Torah, part of the Hebrew Bible, on them

worship   religious ceremony showing love for God

Index